Salvation Incomplete

Salvation Incomplete

Brandon Luna

Copyright © 2016 by Brandon Luna.

Library of Congress Control Number:		2016907827
ISBN:	Hardcover	978-1-5245-0046-7
	Softcover	978-1-5245-0045-0
	eBook	978-1-5245-0044-3

All rights reserved. No part of this book may be reproduced or transmitted in any form or by any means, electronic or mechanical, including photocopying, recording, or by any information storage and retrieval system, without permission in writing from the copyright owner.

Scripture quotations marked NIV are taken from the *Holy Bible, New International Version®. NIV®.* Copyright © 1973, 1978, 1984 by International Bible Society. Used by permission of *Zondervan.* All rights reserved. [*Biblica*]

Scripture quotations marked NKJV are taken from the New King James Version. Copyright © 1982 by *Thomas Nelson, Inc.* Used by permission. All rights reserved.

Scripture quotations marked KJV are from the Holy Bible, King James Version (Authorized Version). First published in 1611. Quoted from the KJV Classic Reference Bible, Copyright © 1983 by The *Zondervan* Corporation.

Any people depicted in stock imagery provided by Thinkstock are models, and such images are being used for illustrative purposes only.
Certain stock imagery © Thinkstock.

Print information available on the last page.

Rev. date: 05/21/2016

To order additional copies of this book, contact:
Xlibris
1-888-795-4274
www.Xlibris.com
Orders@Xlibris.com
739169

CONTENTS

Salvation Incomplete 1
   1. Deductive Argument 1
   2. Connecting Scripture 2
   3. The Confusion Of Works 7
   4. The Prayer Of Salvation 10
   5. The Holy Spirit 11
   6. The Path To Salvation 13

Hearing And Understanding The Word 15
   1. First Soil 16
   2. Second Soil 16
   3. Third Soil 17
   4. Fourth Soil 18

Putting God First And Treating Others Properly 20
   1. Do Not Put Any God Before Me 20
   2. Serving God 21
   3. Individual Spiritual Gifts 22
   4. Morality 23
   5. Behave Like A Christian 23
   6. Forgiving Others 25
   7. Love Your Enemies 26
   8. Judging Others 27

Developing A Relationship With The Lord In Faith 29

1. God Has A Plan For Us All 29
2. God's Timing 29
3. Faith 30
4. Humility 30
5. Ask And You Shall Receive 31
6. Do Not Rely On Your Own Understanding 32
7. Pray About Everything 33

Obedience To The Best Of Our Ability 34

1. Seeking Righteousness 34
2. Deep Repentance 34
3. Learning From Sin 35
4. Don't Put Yourself In Sin's Way 35
5. Strong In The Lord 36

God's Judgment 37

1. Life Is A Mist 37
2. You Will Reap What You Have Sown 37
3. According To Deeds 38
4. Final Judgment 39

SALVATION INCOMPLETE

THE MESSAGE THAT has been given states that reciting the prayer of salvation bestows God's presence among those and the entrance to the kingdom of heaven. This is an incomplete message that leads people to not dedicate themselves to the Lord. There are several scriptures that expose how a sinful life results to eternity in hell.

As a young adult, I would ask fellow Christians and pastors the reason why individuals would speak the prayer of salvation but fail to implement change and Christ-like qualities. The answer would simply always be, "because they are not truly saved." Logically, it didn't make sense to place all of our faith and the future of our eternal soul on a prayer that does not bear the solution to salvation for everyone. It seems that people choose to disobey God even after they say the prayer of salvation. We are given a false sense of security despite the fact that the bible declares effort is needed for eternal life. The truth is that the prayer solely focuses on one aspect of salvation and it is necessary to look further. Since we believe that the Bible is true and there are scriptures that connect to salvation, then we must consider them all in order to adopt an accurate, scripture-based conclusion for salvation.

1. Deductive Argument

A deductive argument is an argument that is intended by the arguer to be (deductively) valid, that is, to provide a guarantee of the truth of the conclusion provided that the argument's premises (assumptions) are true. This point can be expressed also by saying that, in a deductive argument, the premises are intended to provide such strong support for the conclusion that, if the premises are true, then it would be impossible for the conclusion to be false. An argument in which the premises do succeed in guaranteeing the conclusion is called a (deductively) valid argument. If a valid argument has true premises, then the argument is said to be sound.

Example of a Deductive Argument: Premise 1, Premise 2, Conclusion

P1. All dogs are animals.
P2. This is a dog.
C. Therefore, this is an animal.

Basis Of Evidence

P1. The Bible is written Holy Scripture.
P2. The Bible is true.
C. Therefore, the Holy Scripture in the Bible is true.

As Christians, we are basing our faith on the fact that the Holy Scripture in the Bible is true. We would be unable to call ourselves Christians if we failed to come to this conclusion. Therefore, if it is believed that the Holy Scripture is accurate, then respect and validation is needed for all scripture. The Bible possesses scripture that conveys the message that achieving salvation requires accepting Christ. However, this is not the only scripture that pertains to salvation. Because we believe in all of the scripture that coincides with salvation, then we have to connect them all to create a complete conclusion for salvation. If you come to the conclusion that the Holy Scripture in the Bible is true then the scripture becomes undisputable evidence.

2. Connecting Scripture

In order to propose a scripture-based conclusion for salvation, we must connect all scripture that express what is needed in our life to accomplish salvation. If Matthew 6:14 states that we must forgive to be forgiven and we have forgiven everyone who has ever forsaken us throughout our life, but we have stolen and lied without repentance, then we surely cannot go to the Lord on our day of judgment and say, "Lord, Matthew 6:14 states that I must forgive everyone who has forsaken me and I have done so and should be forgiven." I am sure that the Lord will remind us of the sins of the flesh that state that if you make lying and stealing a part of your lifestyle then you will not enter the kingdom of Heaven. This concept is true for salvation as well. The Bible states that there are five aspects needed for eternal life. Believing that Jesus is our Lord and savior, putting God first in your heart, mind and soul, treating others the way you want to be treated, developing a relationship with the Lord in faith, and obedience to the best of our ability. When we only abide in one aspect that scripture says is necessary for salvation but ignore all the other aspects, then our salvation is incomplete.

Believing And Accepting

The first step to salvation is believing and accepting Jesus as your Lord and Savior.

John 3

For God so loved the world, that he gave his only begotten Son, that whosoever believeth in him should not perish, but have everlasting life. **16 KJV**

Romans 10

That if thou shalt confess with thy mouth the Lord Jesus, and shalt believe in thine heart that God hath raised him from the dead, thou shalt be saved. **9 KJV**

These scriptures summarize the prayer of salvation. We must believe that Jesus died for our sins and declare Him as our Lord and savior in order to be saved. However, we have to connect the scriptures that expose the other aspects necessary for eternal life.

God First And Treating Others

The second and third steps are the most important steps to salvation: put God first and hold a good heart. Jesus was asked in Matthew 22 what the greatest commandment was. Jesus replied with two commandments that sum up His law.

Matthew 22
"Teacher, which is the great commandment in the law?" Jesus said to him, "'You shall love the Lord your God with all your heart, with all your soul, and with all your mind.' This is the first and great commandment. 39 And the second is like it: 'You shall love your neighbor as yourself.' On these two commandments hang all the Law and the Prophets." **36-40 NKJV**

Relationship In Faith

The fourth step to salvation is a relationship in faith. God wants to form a relationship with us and guide us through our trials and tribulations. Without a bond, God will not acknowledge you when you call out His name during your judgment.

Matthew 7
Many will say to Me in that day, 'Lord, Lord, have we not prophesied in Your name, cast out demons in Your name, and done many wonders in Your name?' And then I will declare to them, 'I never knew you; depart from Me, you who practice lawlessness!' **22-23 NKJV**

Obedience

James 2
What does it profit, my brethren, if someone says he has faith but does not have works? Can faith save him? If a brother or sister is naked and destitute of daily food, and one of you says to them, "Depart in

peace, be warmed and filled," but you do not give them the things which are needed for the body, what does it profit? Thus also faith by itself, if it does not have works, is dead. **14-17 NKJV**

Hebrews 10

For if we sin willfully after we have received the knowledge of the truth, there no longer remains a sacrifice for sins, **26 NKJV**

Hebrews 10:26 states that if you know the Lord and you deliberately rebel against him in disobedience, the sacrifice of Jesus Christ does not save you.

Furthermore, James 2 reveals that faith without obedience is dead. In Hebrews 10:26, the scripture describes the obedience that is needed to enter the kingdom of Heaven. The works shown in Hebrews 10:26 does not require perfection, but does call us to do our very best to obey the Lord.

Reaching A Conclusion

Now we can connect these Holy Scripture that state that there are more aspects to salvation than believing and accepting Jesus as our savior. If we come to the conclusion that the Holy Scripture in the Bible is true then we can come to a conclusion using scripture based evidence to explain all that is necessary for salvation.

- **P1.** You must believe and accept Jesus as your Lord and savior for salvation. (John 3:16)(Romans 10:9)
- **P2.** Obedience to the best of our ability is necessary for salvation. (James2:18-24, Hebrews 10:26)
- **C.** Therefore, believing and accepting Jesus as your Lord and Savior and following Him in obedience to the best of our ability is necessary for salvation

P1. A relationship with the Lord is necessary for salvation. (Matthew 7:22-23)

P2. Putting God first in your heart, mind and soul, and treating people the way you want to be treated is necessary for salvation. (Matthew 22: 36-40)

C. Therefore, having a relationship with the Lord, putting God first in your heart mind and soul, and treating others the way you want to be treated is necessary for salvation.

We can now combine both deductive conclusions to come to our complete conclusion.

C. Therefore, believing and accepting Jesus as your Lord and savior, putting God first in your heart, mind, and soul, treating others the way you want to be treated, developing a relationship with the Lord in faith, and following the Lord in obedience to the best of our ability is necessary for salvation.

If you believe and come to the conclusion that the Holy Scripture in the Bible is true, then you cannot argue with the complete conclusion. This conclusion is scripture based *evidence*. If you argue with this conclusion then it is a self-contradiction as a Christian. The conclusion is universal and much clearer to what is necessary for eternal life. This conclusion is what should be preached in churches throughout the world because the accuracy will not be hit or miss. As I explained earlier, the prayer of salvation should not be used as a complete solution for eternal salvation, but as the first step in accepting the Holy Spirit and dedication to the Lord. People speak this prayer and the response I receive is that not everyone who says this prayer is truly saved. This is because people choose not to repent even after speaking the prayer. Given the importance of eternal salvation, I believe that the prayer of salvation should no longer be broadcasted as a guarantee for eternal life, but should be placed as the first step in the complete conclusion as the foundation for eternal salvation.

3. The Confusion Of Works

One of the main issues at hand is that people are confused about works. Everyone is stuck on the "Catholic" works for salvation, based on a scale of doing good or bad, or earning salvation through works alone. Since the separation from the Catholic Church, we separated our belief for salvation as well. Now it seems to be the polar opposite of what the Catholic Church believes is necessary for salvation. For most believers common responses are. "By grace we are saved", or "By faith we are saved". If you even mention works it is immediately shot down because of our message that opposes catholic belief. The truth is that effort is necessary for salvation. By connecting scripture, I will be defining exactly which works are necessary for salvation in order to be clear that I am not speaking of works alone.

The Rich Young Man "Works Alone"

Matthew 19

And behold, a man came up to him, saying, "Teacher, what good deed must I do to have eternal life?" And he said to him, "Why do you ask me about what is good? There is only one who is good. If you would enter life, keep the commandments." He said to him, "Which ones?" And Jesus said, "You shall not murder, You shall not commit adultery, You shall not steal, You shall not bear false witness, Honor your father and mother, and, You shall love your neighbor as yourself." The young man said to him, "All these I have kept. What do I still lack?" Jesus said to him, "If you would be perfect, go, sell what you possess and give to the poor, and you will have treasure in heaven; and come, follow me." When the young man heard this he went away sorrowful, for he had great possessions. And Jesus said to his disciples, "Truly, I say to you, only with difficulty will a rich person enter the kingdom of heaven. Again I tell you, it is easier for a camel to go through the eye of a needle than for a rich person to enter the kingdom of God." **16-24 ESV**

According to Jesus, works are not enough to have eternal life. Faith is necessary as well. Moving forward we will see how we will need both faith and works for eternal salvation.

Works Are Necessary To Make Faith Perfect Or Complete

James 2

But someone will say, "You have faith, and I have works." Show me your faith without your works, and I will show you my faith by my works. You believe that there is one God. You do well. Even the demons believe—and tremble! But do you want to know, O foolish man, that faith without works is dead? Was not Abraham our father justified by works when he offered Isaac his son on the altar? Do you see that faith was working together with his works, and by works faith was made perfect? **14-26 NKJV**

Obedience is the works described in James 2 that is necessary. According to scripture, Abraham's faith was incomplete and imperfect without obedience. When he followed God in obedience, then his faith was made perfect.

Obedience To The Best Of Our Ability

Hebrews 10

For if we sin willfully after we have received the knowledge of the truth, there no longer remains a sacrifice for sins, **26 NKJV**

We can see in Hebrews 10:26 is where the issue lies. The idea of works for salvation is defined as:

Works- earning Salvation through good deeds and a lack of sin.

The works that are necessary for salvation is defined as follows-

Works- Obedience to the best of our ability.

We are not asked to be perfect, but we must keep in mind that obedience to the best of our ability is the "works" necessary to be forgiven. This is exactly where the confusion lies. Once again connecting these scripture we can see that faith and works are both necessary. We can also see that by works alone are not enough for salvation, but that obedience to the best of our ability makes your faith perfect.

Sinful Lifestyle

Galatians 5

Now the works of the flesh are evident, which are: adultery, fornication, uncleanness, lewdness, idolatry, sorcery, hatred, contentions, jealousies, outbursts of wrath, selfish ambitions, dissensions, heresies, envy, murders, drunkenness, revelries, and the like; of which I tell you beforehand, just as I also told you in time past, that those who practice such things will not inherit the kingdom of God. **19-21 NKJV**

Hebrews 10:26 and the word practice in Galatians 5:21 indicate that sin that is not forgiven is more of a lifestyle choice. This does not include a Christian who is seeking righteousness that slips up and has one too many drinks. This pinpoints the confusion of works.

We can now come to the conclusion that works are necessary for salvation and if you ask for forgiveness, then you will have it, as long as you don't go on deliberately living a sinful lifestyle. God will forgive us if we disobey. We all have our time of weakness and no one is perfect, but we cannot deliberately sin or live in sin.

Complete Conclusion.
- C. Therefore, believing and accepting Jesus as your Lord and savior, putting God first in your heart, mind, and soul, treating others the way you want to be treated, developing a relationship with the Lord in faith, and following the Lord in obedience to the best of our ability is necessary for salvation.

4. The Prayer Of Salvation

An argument for the prayer of salvation that I always hear is that it will give the Holy Spirit and eternal life to those who speak it. There is no need for any other action because the Holy Spirit will change you and you will make Christ like decisions. At the same time, when you ask people about those who have not changed, the response is that the individual is not truly saved. This means that according to the argument, they didn't receive the Holy Spirit and eternal salvation regardless of the fact that they prayed the prayer of salvation. Going further, they say that this person didn't truly mean it when saying the prayer and that is why they didn't receive the Holy Spirit and are not truly saved. First of all, when saying the prayer of salvation, I believe that we all have the same intention, which is to accept the Holy Spirit and attain eternal salvation. At that moment, we all have every intention of receiving the Holy Spirit in our lives. Secondly, the argument given for the prayer of salvation is known as an inconsistency fallacy.

The inconsistency fallacy is an argument that includes a contradiction. The argument is flawed due to the fact that two distinct beliefs are both promoted. In other words, the claims are inconsistent with one another.

Example
- **P1.** Everyone and only some people love football
- **P2.** Everyone loves football.
- **C.** Therefore football is loved by everyone.

Argument For The Prayer Of Salvation

- **P1.** Saying the prayer of salvation gives everyone and only some people who speak it the Holy Spirit and eternal salvation.
- **P2.** The prayer of salvation gives everyone the Holy Spirit and eternal salvation.
- **C.** Therefore everyone who says the prayer of salvation receives the Holy Spirit and eternal salvation.

Since the conclusion is considered logically inconstant or a logical fallacy based on inconsistency, then the conclusion can be labeled as false.

The prayer of salvation is produced by Romans 10: 9 and John 3:16. According to the message received, if we say this prayer, then we will be saved and it is guaranteed that you will have eternal life. The prayer is not a complete solution according to scripture so we cannot use it as evangelists. There are many who do not have a relationship with God, and decide not to repent following the "prayer of salvation". I have personally witnessed many people with substantial problems in their life pray the prayer of salvation, change for a split moment, and then fall back into the lifestyle they were in before. Not one piece of scripture states that we should say a prayer and that is the end of our journey to salvation. What would be the need for the Lord to continue to test us, if we had no ability to turn from the Lord after accepting the Holy Spirit and proclaiming Jesus as our Lord and Savior? The Lord calls the Church Body His Bride; so look at the prayer of salvation the same as marriage vows. If you unite in marriage and proclaim that you will be faithful yet you are unfaithful, commit adultery, and choose sin over your marriage, then your wife has a right to divorce you. This is the same concept as the prayer of salvation. If you have proclaimed Jesus your Lord and Savior and then go on living a sinful life, then you will not enjoy eternity with Him. This is the truth. Based on Holy Scripture, declaring to the Lord that you believe and you accept Him as your Lord and Savior is not enough.

5. The Holy Spirit

Acts 2
"Repent ye, and be baptized every one of you in the name of Jesus Christ unto the remission of your sins; and ye shall receive the gift of the Holy Spirit" **38 ASV**

John 14

But the Advocate, the Holy Spirit, whom the Father will send in my name, will teach you all things and will remind you of everything I have said to you. **26 NIV**

Romans 8

Likewise the Spirit helps us in our weakness. For we do not know what to pray for as we ought, but the Spirit himself intercedes for us with groanings too deep for words. And he who searches hearts knows what is the mind of the Spirit, because the Spirit intercedes for the saints according to the will of God. **26-27 ESV**

According to these scriptures, you must come to the Lord and receive the Holy Spirit. From there, you will have access to the Holy Spirit or He will intercede according to the will of God. The Holy Spirit is a gift and our helper, as stated in scripture. Scriptures do not describe the Holy Spirit as a decision maker. He is more of an assistant; there for help if you need Him. The message given to us is that there is no effort needed on our part because the Holy Spirit will change us to become repentant. We will always have the free will to choose sin or obedience even after receiving the Holy Spirit. The Lord gives us the Holy Spirit, not to be possessed by him to make our decisions for us, but to help us on our path. If we make the decisions that are in accordance to the will of God, the Holy Spirit will be there to help guide us. The Holy Spirit will help us remember scripture, help us in prayer, help us in repentance, will soften our hearts, and transform us if we allow Him to. Romans 8 states that the Holy Spirit intercedes for the Saints, not the rebellious sinners - so it will be up to you to repent, and when you make that decision, the Holy Spirit will be there to guide you. However, you will not be forced to repent. The Holy Spirit will not force you to continue repenting once you have initially decided to. With the help you receive, the Holy Spirit will help you in transforming yourself. We cannot change without the Holy Spirit, but we can choose how much help we receive based on the effort we put into being as Christ-like as we possibly can be.

6. The Path To Salvation

Proverbs 4

Let your eyes look straight ahead; fix your gaze directly before you. Give careful thought to the paths for your feet and be steadfast in all your ways. Do not turn to the right or the left; keep your foot from evil. **25-27 NIV**

Matthew 7

"Enter by the narrow gate. For the gate is wide and the way is easy that leads to destruction, and those who enter by it are many. For the gate is narrow and the way is hard that leads to life, and those who find it are few. **13-14 ESV**

Proverbs 4

They eat the bread of wickedness and drink the wine of violence. The path of the righteous is like the morning sun, shining ever brighter till the full light of day. But the way of the wicked is like deep darkness; they do not know what makes them stumble. **17-19 NIV**

Salvation is accomplished based on the path that you have decided to walk on throughout your life. If you choose the path that leads to salvation then you will have your eternal life, but if you have spent your life on the path of destruction, then you will be separated from the Lord for eternity. Very few choose the path that leads to eternal life. These few have made a decision to make their eternity a priority in their lives. They are successful based on what truly matters and invest in eternal riches. They treat others the way they want to be treated and understand what life is truly about.

If you are willing to accept sin into your life and believe that because you have said the prayer of salvation and received the Holy Spirit you will not be turned away during judgment, then you are not on the path of salvation. You will always run into dead ends and never find or fulfill your purpose on this path. If you are on the path of righteousness then you will be led by the Holy Spirit to get every aspect of sin out of your life. Even though it is impossible to completely stop sinning, the path of righteousness is a lifetime journey of repentance with the hope that in time you will become as close to imitating Jesus Christ as possible. This is a choice that we should be putting in front of us every day. We follow the Lord in faith and learn to love Him. Once you have developed a relationship with him and fall in love with your Father then it will be hard to wander away. You cannot fall off the path of righteousness by sinning. You can, though, by making sin a part of your life without repentance. The path of righteousness includes doing your best to put God first in every action that you take, in every thought you have and loving the Lord with all of your heart - very few are on it. Consider this if you have sin that you have not repented because you are comfortable in thinking that you will be forgiven without repentance. Make the changes necessary and walk through the narrow gate.

HEARING AND UNDERSTANDING THE WORD

I HAVE WITNESSED to many, and the first step to salvation for everyone is hearing the truth and comprehending it. The scripture that best describes this is-

The Parable Of The Sower

Matthew 13

That same day Jesus went out of the house and sat by the lake. Such large crowds gathered around him that he got into a boat and sat in it, while all the people stood on the shore. Then he told them many things in parables, saying: "A farmer went out to sow his seed. As he was scattering the seed, some fell along the path, and the birds came and ate it up. Some fell on rocky places, where it did not have much soil. It sprang up quickly, because the soil was shallow. But when the sun came up, the plants were scorched, and they withered because they had no root. Other seed fell among thorns, which grew up and choked the plants. Still other seed fell on good soil, where it produced a crop—a hundred, sixty or thirty times what was sown. Whoever has ears, let them hear."

The disciples came to him and asked, "Why do you speak to the people in parables?"

He replied, "Because the knowledge of the secrets of the kingdom of heaven has been given to you, but not to them. Whoever has will be given more, and they will have an abundance. Whoever does not have, even what they have will be taken from them. This is why I speak to them in parables:

"Though seeing, they do not see; though hearing, they do not hear or understand. In them is fulfilled the prophecy of Isaiah:

"'You will be ever hearing but never understanding, you will be ever seeing but never perceiving. For this people's heart has become calloused; they hardly hear with their ears, and they have closed their eyes. Otherwise they might see with their eyes, hear with their ears, understand with their hearts and turn, and I would heal them.

But blessed are your eyes because they see, and your ears because they hear. For truly I tell you, many prophets and righteous people longed to see what you see but did not see it, and to hear what you hear but did not hear it.

"Listen then to what the parable of the sower means: When anyone hears the message about the kingdom and does not understand it, the evil one comes and snatches away what was sown in their heart. This is the seed sown along the path. The seed falling on rocky ground refers to someone who hears the word and at once receives it with joy. But since they have no root, they last only a short time. When trouble or persecution comes because of the word, they quickly fall away. The seed falling among the thorns refers to someone who hears the word, but the worries of this life and the deceitfulness of wealth choke the word, making it unfruitful. But the seed falling on good soil refers to someone who hears the word and understands it. This is the one who produces a crop, yielding a hundred, sixty or thirty times what was sown." **1-23 NIV**

Examine yourself and put yourself in the category that pertains to you.

1. First Soil

The first soil was never affected by the Lord. They hear the word and don't understand. They continue living for this world in the here and now.

2. Second Soil

The second soil is happy to receive the word and is grateful that you have shared the word with them. Meanwhile, the Devil, who is happy to leave you alone when you are on the wrong path, takes notice when you try to make a change. A friend that I had witnessed to told me that after accepting the Word, there were girls that he hadn't heard from in years calling him up and pulling him into sin. He turned his back on the Lord only months after receiving the truth.

3. Third Soil

In my opinion, the third soil represents a majority of the world. When there are uncomfortable situations in your life, the first response is to worry. The Lord says to cast your worries out to Him and he will answer your prayers, however, it is hard to stay calm and look for purpose in your suffering. It is hard to consider our conditioning pure joy. The point is to surrender completely to the Lord, and the more you surrender to the Lord, the happier you become. Living in faith, you don't have to worry about this world. The Lord loves us more than we can imagine and he has more thoughts about us than there are grains of sand.

Psalm 139

How precious also are thy thoughts unto me, O God! how great is the sum of them! If I should count them, they are more in number than the sand: when I awake, I am still with thee. **17-18 KJV**

We were not created to fail, to be homeless and shamed as followers of God. Consider the birds.

Matthew 6

Look at the birds of the air; they do not sow or reap or store away in barns, and yet your heavenly Father feeds them. Are you not much more valuable than they? **26 NIV**

There is not a worry large enough that our Lord, that created the ground that you walk on and the air that you breathe, cannot handle. Surrender all to Him and allow yourself to live your life.

The deception of wealth is strong in this world. Who doesn't want to have nice things? I'm sure that we have all seen the reality shows with people living pointless lives. It is obvious that these people are unhappy. The truth of the matter is that wealth is temporary. Wealth is a misconception of what success truly is. Worldly success is based on how wealthy we are. A big house, nice car, and a beautiful wife is what is important in this world. Investing in knowing the Lord and loving his law makes a successful life in truth. What good is it to gain the whole world but lose your soul? If you are broken, will a house cause you to be whole? If your heart needs love will a car give it to you? Cars, houses, and toys will all fall apart in time, but investing in the Lord is eternal.

4. Fourth Soil

The fourth soil is the wise soil; understanding what is important in life. It is wise enough to know the repercussions of the decisions in this life and understanding eternity. Life is a mist – our life is so short in comparison to eternity. It is a short breath in our existence. A young man asked me why we live in this world and why we don't live in heaven with God. It was actually a very important question that we all need to understand. We exist here on earth with our clock ticking away, and every day we make a choice. Will we serve God or serve Satan? According to the scripture we are serving whoever we obey.

1 Peter 3

Don't you know that when you offer yourselves to someone as obedient slaves, you are slaves of the one you obey--whether you are slaves to sin, which leads to death, or to obedience, which leads to righteousness? **16 NIV**

From the beginning of time we all have had the freedom to choose; the angels had their choice, and a third of them followed Satan. The choices we make are in accordance to what we consider to be important in our lives. The fourth soil understands what is truly important in life and is dedicated to success in their eternal life.

The Fourth Soil produces crop thirty, sixty or one hundred fold, depending on the person. When you allow the Lord to take the lead in your life and not have the worries of the third soil, then you have peace in your life to spread the word of God. The other soils are caught up in the world and too busy with it to have time for the Lord.

PUTTING GOD FIRST AND TREATING OTHERS PROPERLY

1. Do Not Put Any God Before Me

PUTTING GOD FIRST is a matter of asking yourself what is most important in life. Because of this, people put effort into what is most important to them. I have seen people practically kill themselves to get college degrees. How many hours of studying does it take to get a masters degree in business? People have their goals in life wrapped around their jobs to get worldly possession. The question is, how much time and effort do you spend on developing a relationship with the lord? Loving the Lord with all of your heart, mind, and soul and treating others the way you want to be treated are the two most important things in this life. So why is our relationship with God down on our list of importance? Consider a Master Sommelier, these people are masters of wine. There are only about 200 in the world and it takes at least six years of consistent studying to get to the point of being able to identify the vineyard, year the wine was made, and the producer of the wine they are tasting with just a sniff and a taste. This is one of many aspects of this test and very few can become Master Sommeliers. Many people have sacrificed much of their time and life in dedication to this title. Many constantly studied for years and never attain this title. Only ten percent pass the final exam and I guarantee that the individuals that have earned the title of Master Sommelier made it the most important thing in their life. Take some time to evaluate what is most important to you. We must dedicate our life to the lord and become masters of living a Christian life. In every action we take, we must put the Lord into consideration. We must be relentless in our consideration of God's will in our life. In our heart, mind, and soul. In constant thought of God. In every action considering God and loving God's law because it is best intended for our good and in constant thought of how close to perfection we can become. How hard are you willing to work to become an image of Christ in this life? How many hours of prayer and dedication have you sacrificed to the Lord? Dedication is needed for eternal salvation. A dedication in consideration of what is truly important - God's will.

2. Serving God

Serving God is not one dimensional. Many believe that service in the Lord is volunteering or serving in missions. These are ways that you physically serve the Lord but we must live in service of the Lord as Christians.

When your boss asks you to do something for them, you cannot tell them that you don't have time for that or that you have other plans. If you want to keep your job, it is necessary to do what your boss asks of you. When you obey your boss, it is for the service of the company at whole. This is the same concept for the Lord. When we have a decision to make and the devil is trying to pull us into sin, then we have a decision in service to make.

1 Peter 3

Don't you know that when you offer yourselves to someone as obedient slaves, you are slaves of the one you obey--whether you are slaves to sin, which leads to death, or to obedience, which leads to righteousness? **16 NIV**

Understand that every decision you make is in service to our Father or in Satan. Hate in any degree is in service of Satan. From a discouraging comment all the way up to murder is considered hateful and of service to Satan. Love in any degree is in service of the Lord. A smile or a hug all the way up to sacrificing your life for someone. Jesus showed us unconditional love by giving his life for us. Your actions are service. Your actions are your fruit in this life. You will be known by your fruit.

3. Individual Spiritual Gifts

Romans 12

For by the grace given me I say to every one of you: Do not think of yourself more highly than you ought, but rather think of yourself with sober judgment, in accordance with the faith God has distributed to each of you. For just as each of us has one body with many members, and these members do not all have the same function, so in Christ we, though many, form one body, and each member belongs to all the others. We have different gifts, according to the grace given to each of us. If your gift is prophesying, then prophesy in accordance with your faith; if it is serving, then serve; if it is teaching, then teach; if it is to encourage, then give encouragement; if it is giving, then give generously; if it is to lead, do it diligently; if it is to show mercy, do it cheerfully. **3-9 NIV**

Each of us are different but can be categorized into different personality types and have gifts given by God to serve Him and help each other. A salesman has good interpersonal communication skills and would be good in serving the Lord by speaking in front of others. A mechanic is less personable but would be a great asset doing hands on mission work. The thought that most of us have is that the Lord has given us these gifts to earn money. You do have to make money to survive in this world but above the work we do for our family and the money we earn; the true purpose is that the Lord has given us these gifts in hope that we will all work together to help one another and to serve Him. Imagine if the entire world was serving God together as one church body. Consider if our churches were united in service to the Lord. Churches should be communicating with each other for all service to the Lord to have more of an effect in communities and on missions. The church body is separated from itself. Let us stand up and unite for the purpose of serving. A revival is needed in these end days. Do your part in contribution for a solution in service to Christ so the Church Body can be whole and functioning to the best of its ability.

4. Morality

God is constant in His word. If law in this world states that smoking marijuana and gambling is legal then is it morally correct even though it is a sin? If your family is judgmental but scripture states that you cannot be judgmental, then is it good form to do the same? Will you follow the Lord and His law or will you conform to the world? The world accepts sin in every form and the goal is to get each and every one of us to accept sin in our lives so that we spend eternity separated from the Lord. You cannot place your morality in the hands of the world. Place eternal acceptance above earthly acceptance.

5. Behave Like A Christian

There is a certain way that God asks us to act as Christians. Our goal is to treat others the way we want to be treated.

Romans 12

Love must be sincere. Hate what is evil; cling to what is good. Be devoted to one another in love. Honor one another above yourselves. Never be lacking in zeal, but keep your spiritual fervor, serving the Lord. Be joyful in hope, patient in affliction, faithful in prayer. Share with the Lord's people who are in need. Practice hospitality. Bless those who persecute you; bless and do not curse. Rejoice with those who rejoice; mourn with those who mourn. Live in harmony with one another. Do not be proud, but be willing to associate with people of low position. Do not be conceited. Do not repay anyone evil for evil. Be careful to do what is right in the eyes of everyone. If it is possible, as far as it depends on you, live at peace with everyone. Do not take revenge, my dear friends, but leave room for God's wrath, for it is written: "It is mine to avenge; I will repay," says the Lord. On the contrary:

"If your enemy is hungry, feed him;
if he is thirsty, give him something to drink.
In doing this, you will heap burning coals on his head."
Do not be overcome by evil, but overcome evil with good.
9-21 NIV

In each interaction with someone, you have a decision to make – you can be nice or not. Under handed comments and passive aggressive behavior is not nice. It is just a way of hiding your ugliness. Regardless if it is considered less hateful, it is still in service of Satan. You are responsible for the effect you have on the people you come across. If you are hateful to others and then call yourself a Christian, then you have a decision to make; you can stop calling yourself a Christian and continue being hateful, or you can start representing the Lord properly. It is tiring to witness to the people of this world and invite them to attend church, only to receive a response that Christians are judgmental and rude. I had a friend in the Marine Corps that went to a church where he said everyone was rude to him because he smoked a cigarette in the parking lot. He never went back to church and most likely won't ever go back again. He was reaching out for the Lord and in his eyes, the people of this church represent the Lord. He needed the Lord Just like everyone else and these "Christians" were rude. How can I witness to him when he now sees our Lord as rude and judgmental? Let me tell all of you something: if a homeless man off the street wants to come into the church you attend, then I guarantee you that it is the will of God for him to be there. The Church you attend is not "your Church"- it is the House of the Lord. It doesn't belong to you, so when you're in church, act according to God's will or don't come at all. If you decide that you will not consider others feelings or emotions, then you are a part of the problem here on earth. Consider these two words.

Encourage- to inspire with courage, spirit, or confidence
Discourage- to deprive of courage, hope, or confidence; dishearten; dispirit.

When you discourage someone we can see that it deprives them of courage, confidence, and hope. Discouragement could lead people to drug or alcohol abuse. Discouragement could lead people to depression or suicide. The devil likes us to think about our mistakes and issues. He likes us to think about the reasons why we aren't good enough, so that we will be discouraged and not have the courage and confidence to fulfill God's purpose for us. Discouragement is Satan's work. If you are discouraging people in this life, you need to repent. If you decide that you are going to continue these actions, then don't call yourself a Christian because when you are turned away by the Lord, your punishment will not be as severe. Also, people of this world will not be confused about who true Christians are. Everyone will say, "If I need help, I can talk to a Christian. They are always encouraging."

On the other hand, people in distress give us a chance to lead as Christians in encouragement. When is the last time someone came to you with an issue or a problem and you encouraged them through the Lord? It is one of the purposes that you have in this life to encourage others with love and let them know that the love that they are receiving is from the Lord. You don't have to be well versed in scripture to let someone know that the Lord loves them and He is waiting to hear from them so that He can help them through their life. Giving someone confidence and hope is the will of God for everyone. Comforting the ones you know with love and compassion can change them forever.

6. Forgiving Others

Matthew 6

"For if you forgive men their trespasses, your heavenly Father will also forgive you. But if you do not forgive men their trespasses, neither will your Father forgive your trespasses. **14-15 NKJV**

Treating others the way you want to be treated sums up the law of God. While you are being judged, you will understand why it is so important to treat others the way you want to be treated in every aspect of your life. If you are unforgiving then you will not be forgiven. You will reap what you have sown; if we all make mistakes and don't forgive others that sin against you then unforgiving judgment is what you have sown. We have all made mistakes and I'm sure that we all would want to be forgiven with love for the mistakes that we have made. This is why our Heavenly Father is willing to forgive us as long as we are willing to be loving as well and treat others as we would want to be treated. The Lord created us, and instead of putting his law first in everything we do, we blatantly disrespect the Lord, over and over again. We want to be forgiven but have chosen not to forgive people that have forsaken us. People have their peaks and valleys; when you find out someone has made a mistake and you tell them that you love and forgive them instead of condemnation and hate, it could make a positive change in that person. They will say, "This Christian is loving and forgiving. How can I have that kind of peace in my life?

7. Love Your Enemies

Matthew 5

You have heard that it was said, Love your neighbor and hate your enemy. But I tell you, love your enemies and pray for those who persecute you, that you may be children of your Father in heaven. He causes his sun to rise on the evil and the good, and sends rain on the righteous and the unrighteous. If you love those who love you, what reward will you get? Are not even the tax collectors doing that? And if you greet only your own people, what are you doing more than others? Do not even pagans do that? Be perfect, therefore, as your heavenly Father is perfect. **43-48 NIV**

I met a man who was doing prison ministry. One of the inmates came up to him and spat in his face. Instead of reacting, he wiped his face and continued reading scripture, still in complete peace with the Lord. The inmate apologized and gave his life to the Lord that day because of the man's forgiveness and love for him regardless of the blatant disrespect. The goal is to find love and wisdom; understanding that we are all imperfect, we are all guilty, and we must have a loving heart and pray for those who have forsaken you.

8. Judging Others

Romans 2

Therefore you have no excuse, O man, every one of you who judges. For in passing judgment on another you condemn yourself, because you, the judge, practice the very same things. We know that the judgment of God rightly falls on those who practice such things. Do you suppose, O man—you who judge those who practice such things and yet do them yourself—that you will escape the judgment of God? Or do you presume on the riches of his kindness and forbearance and patience, not knowing that God's kindness is meant to lead you to repentance? But because of your hard and impenitent heart you are storing up wrath for yourself on the day of wrath when God's righteous judgment will be revealed. He will render to each one according to his works: to those who by patience in well-doing seek for glory and honor and immortality, he will give eternal life; but for those who are self-seeking and do not obey the truth, but obey unrighteousness, there will be wrath and fury. **1-8 ESV**

I would like to start off by saying that I love how this scripture is explaining how God's judgment is fair and righteous in verse two. By stating that "therefore you have no excuse" it is explaining that you are absolutely responsible for your actions. When scripture states that you must treat others the way you want to be treated, this might not have been an example you have thought of in this life. If you are judgmental in this life, then you are condemning yourself. Because you have judged others in condemnation, you are guilty of the sin of judgment. You will hear judgmental people say things such as, "Can you believe what they did?" giving themselves a feeling of superiority and forgetting about their sin. Every time you condemn others when they do wrong, you are setting yourself up to be judged the same way. If you aren't perfect then I would be mindful of your judgment towards others.

Matthew 7

"Judge not, that you be not judged. For with what judgment you judge, you will be judged; and with the measure you use, it will be measured back to you. And why do you look at the speck in your brother's eye, but do not consider the plank in your own eye? **1-3 NKJV**

I have met and seen many people condemn others in judgment, in an egotistical, rude fashion as if God put them in a position of judgment because of their Christian report card. Matthew 7 states that if you are partaking in this behavior, you will be judged in the same fashion that you are judging others. Due to the fact that no one in this world is perfect besides Jesus Christ Himself, the lesson is not to make others feel bad in their time of weakness but to encourage them because we are all sinners. Unless you want to be condemned for your wrong doings for eternity, you should treat others the way you want to be treated.

DEVELOPING A RELATIONSHIP WITH THE LORD IN FAITH

1. God Has A Plan For Us All

CONSIDER THIS: COULD it be possible that God has a vision for us to serve Him and for us to live in complete happiness, but most of us have not allowed God to lead us to our purpose? As the third soil, many have been so consumed with the world that we have not focused on the life that God has for us. The only thing holding us back from our purpose being revealed to us is our faith.

2. God's Timing

2 Peter 3

But, beloved, be not ignorant of this one thing, that one day is with the Lord as a thousand years, and a thousand years as one day. **8 KJV**

Acts 1

He said to them: "It is not for you to know the times or dates the Father has set by his own authority. **7 NIV**

Time was created by the Lord for this world; we are all living in a world of seconds, days, months, and years that pass by. Time is something that weighs on all of us. We will not be restricted by time in the next life; we will be living without time and the feeling of eternity that is described in 2 Peter. God lives in a constant existence of eternity. He knows what you want and knows when you want it. He will not give you your blessings according to your timing but will be looking at your troubles from an outsider's perspective. He will allow your blessings and answer your prayers according to eternal timing and understanding. If you are asking for help with your finances because you are struggling every month to pay your bills and just scraping by, the Lord might not answer your prayers for two years. He will wait for you to learn and grow while He has the exact time that you are meant to receive what the Lord has for you. It is easy to become impatient with the Lord and His timing but the point is to understand that you will exist forever and have faith that the Lord will be there for you. Consider your life. Do you remember when you were a child? It seems like a blink and now we are adults. Consider how quickly those years went by. This is how we understand eternity. Eternity is the timing that our Lord considers for us. A blink is like a thousand years. Be patient in the Lord, He is in constant thought of you and your troubles. Live in faith.

3. Faith

Abraham had the faith to know that the Lord loves him and knows what is best for him. He decided to follow the Lord in obedience when asked to sacrifice his son regardless of the fact that his son's death is the last thing that he wanted in his life. He knew and developed a relationship with the Lord to the point of understanding that the Lord wouldn't steer him in the wrong direction. Faith is stepping out and following the Lord even though you don't know what will happen in the future. Since Abraham was willing to obey the Lord when tested, the Lord made him a father of many in return. This is a lesson that we all need to understand. A relationship in faith is needed for salvation and will lead us to our purpose and blessings.

4. Humility

A relationship with the Lord starts with humility in prayer. Humble yourself in prayer and allow the Lord to lead your life according to His understanding.

Matthew 18

And Jesus called a little child unto him, and set him in the midst of them, And said, Verily I say unto you, Except ye be converted, and become as little children, ye shall not enter into the kingdom of heaven. **2-3 KJV**

In order to become like a child, we must consider their attributes in order to achieve eternal life. A child is joyful, loving, kind, and forgiving. A child doesn't worry about this world because they have faith their parents will provide everything that is needed and keep them safe. A child is obedient and listens to their parents. As this relates to us in God's guidance, I picture a young boy holding his father's hand in the park. The boy has no idea how to get back home or take care of himself. The boy is completely humble and filled with faith that his father will guide him, help him make decisions, feed and take care of him. If there is a problem in his life, he has faith that his father will resolve it for him. Take your Heavenly Father's hand and let Him take control of your life. Humble yourself like a child and pray to your Lord.

Jesus was humble enough to allow our Holy Father to guide Him to be crucified. He was spit on and humiliated for our good. Jesus was a carpenter; he didn't care about the size of his house or wearing fashionable clothing, nor did He ask to sit on a throne. He is our Savior, the Son of God, and He washed the feet of His disciples. He didn't abuse His power to serve Himself. Imagine if our Lord was boastful and had selfish thoughts in mind. In this world's history we have seen the kings who have abused their power and caused horror on earth. The Lord created us and every day we choose to sin in defiance. Instead of an unforgiving Lord who could become angry and send us all to hell, He has decided to sacrifice His son Jesus, who dedicated His life to helping others and spreading love throughout the world. We are truly lucky to have such a loving God to serve.

5. Ask And You Shall Receive

Matthew 8

And behold, there arose a great storm on the sea, so that the boat was being swamped by the waves; but he was asleep. And they went and woke him, saying, "Save us, Lord; we are perishing." And he said to them, "Why are you afraid, O you of little faith?" Then he rose and rebuked the winds and the sea, and there was a great calm. And the men marveled, saying, "What sort of man is this, that even winds and sea obey him?" **24-27 ESV**

The Scripture is explaining that if you are experiencing a storm in your life and you don't ask God for help then He will not intervene until you pray for assistance. He also is explaining that He is waiting for you to humble yourself and turn to Him so He can be there for you. Consider how you feel when you ask a neighbor for help. You don't want to obligate someone with the burdens of your life. You don't want to be in a vulnerable position, with a possibility of feeling dejected if your neighbor says "no can't help you." The Lord sees these types of situations as a possibility to develop a relationship with you. He welcomes your worries and issues. Why are you afraid? The Lord is with you as soon as you call on Him.

6. Do Not Rely On Your Own Understanding

Planning for your future is something that is considered "smart." It is easy to plan and want the best for ourselves. The Lord created us and has a plan for us. The job of a Christian is to allow the Lord to show you your path. What I've learned through leaning on the Lord to write all of the chapters in my book of life, is that as much as you work towards a goal or have an idea on how you want to live your life, the Lord will always have something better for you that will give you more fulfillment. God has a plan for us that fits the personality that the Lord has given us.

God has created us and knows every detail of who we are including the number of hairs on our head. If the Lord has you in a position where you need guidance, then guidance is what you should ask for. If you're in a position that you're not happy in then you can ask to be removed in this situation and be placed in a better one. When closing up prayers of guidance, you must end with "let your will be done." If you pray to be removed from a situation and you remain in it, then the Lord has a reason for your suffering. Focus on the lesson that the Lord is trying to teach and from there He will have another plan for you. If you don't grow from the circumstances that you are in then the Lord might not remove your from it until you have grown.

When you have said a prayer, have the faith in understanding that there will be an answer. You will have to look for the answer and once it is given to you then it will be very clear.

7. Pray About Everything

Once you have a close relationship with the Lord, then you will begin to constantly pray. When things are good, give your gratitude to the Lord. When things are bad, ask for help. When someone needs help, pray that the Lord reaches out to them. When you need direction, ask the Lord for guidance. There is not an issue too large or an issue too small that He will not be able to handle. Be in constant prayer and the Lord will be close to you.

OBEDIENCE TO THE BEST OF OUR ABILITY

1. Seeking Righteousness

WHAT DOES IT mean to seek the Lord? As I see it, a seeker of the Lord wants to know the Lord, follows the Lord's commandments, discusses the Lord, wants an intimate relationship with the Lord, and turns to the Lord for every aspect of their life. Our goal is to be as close to perfection as we can get in the Lord's eyes. Jesus showed us the way and we must strive for it as Christians. We cannot be satisfied knowing we have forgiveness.

Hebrews 10
For if we sin willfully after we have received the knowledge of the truth, there no longer remains a sacrifice for sins, **26 NKJV**

If we sin purposely then we have no sacrifice. Knowing this we have to examine ourselves and come into deep repentance.

2. Deep Repentance

How does God want us to conduct ourselves? We have to look at all of the aspects of what the Lord expects from us so we don't fall into a sinful lifestyle and end up separated from Him forever. We must humble ourselves and ask the Lord where we are falling short. He will show you all of your ways. When you have seen your flaws, you then have to do your best to change. This is hard for everyone, but with the Lord anything is possible. If there is a particular sin that you have made a habit out of, then these will be harder to break. Although, If your salvation is important to you then you will push through. I have personally broken daily habits that were very hard to break. Breaking habits will generally go as follows: The first week, you will most likely slip up once or twice. The second week, possibly once. From there, maybe once or twice a month. Finally, it gets to the point where this sin will occur once every few months until you lose your taste completely for that particular sin. It is very important to understand our downfalls and try to overcome them to the best of your ability.

3. Learning From Sin

Sin happens for a reason and there are different ways that God tests us. There is always a lesson to be learned in everything, even when we sin. If you can look for an answer directly after sinning and understand that God has a purpose for these moments in your life, then you have truly accomplished wisdom. Every time you sin, look for a solution based on how you sinned in the first place. Try and understand what caused you to sin so that you can understand the source of the sin and try to stop the sin before it begins. If we go on sinning without looking for a solution to the sin, we will never have one. For example, if you have a problem with your temper, God might put some very frustrating situations in your path knowing that you will fail. This is God testing you and hoping that you will look to Him for guidance to find a solution to this problem. Once you pray and ask the Lord for a solution, He will give you wisdom and allow you to use the solution He has for you in future frustrating situations.

4. Don't Put Yourself In Sin's Way

Proverbs 5

My son, be attentive to my wisdom, incline your ear to my understanding, that you may keep discretion, and your lips may guard knowledge. For the lips of a forbidden woman drip honey, and her speech is smoother than oil, but in the end she is bitter as wormwood, sharp as a two-edged sword. Her feet go down to death; her steps follow the path to Sheol; she does not ponder the path of life; her ways wander, and she does not know it. And now, O sons, listen to me, and do not depart from the words of my mouth. Keep your way far from her, and do not go near the door of her house. **1-8 ESV**

If you associate yourself with drug addicts then eventually you will become a drug addict. If you are married and you decide to spend your time in bars with women who have no sense of morality, then you will lose your sense of morality and sin will get in the way of your marriage.

5. Strong In The Lord

The decisions we make have a ripple effect. We are all accountable for our decisions. Not only are we accountable for ourselves, but also for the effect we have on others. For example, if a married father of three gets a promotion and starts making money, then suddenly, younger and more attractive women are interested in this married man, he has a decision to make that will effect many people. If he decides to leave his wife and children in order to follow his selfish ways, he is causing pain and suffering to his wife and children. The effect that this has on his wife and children could cause them so much pain that it could alter their ability to perform the purpose that the Lord has for them. This example can relate to women as well, if your husband loses his job, that does not mean it is time to give up on your marriage. Anyone can make the wrong decisions, but it takes a true Christian to make the right ones. Anyone can sin. It doesn't make you a man to drink and have sex like the rest of the world. Real men have the courage to stand up and keep their honor according to the Law of the Lord.

GOD'S JUDGMENT

1. Life Is A Mist

James 4

Why, you do not even know what will happen tomorrow. What is your life? You are a mist that appears for a little while and then vanishes. **14 NIV**

Life moves by so quickly and before you know it we will all be held accountable for our lives. According to scripture, the Lord is fair. From accounts of individuals who have had near death experiences and have actually been judged by the Lord, He will be showing you every moment of your life. He will be explaining what you have done right and what you have done wrong. According to scripture, there will be no one to push blame on and there are no excuses. In these moments it will be clear how much you have understood what is truly important in your life. This can be a very good experience or the beginning of a very bad one.

2. You Will Reap What You Have Sown

Galatians 6

Do not be deceived: God is not mocked, for whatever one sows, that will he also reap. For the one who sows to his own flesh will from the flesh reap corruption, but the one who sows to the Spirit will from the Spirit reap eternal life. And let us not grow weary of doing good, for in due season we will reap, if we do not give up. So then, as we have opportunity, let us do good to everyone, and especially to those who are of the household of faith. **7-10 ESV**

I think it is interesting how in my opinion we have all been deceived to believe that God's judgment will not be placed on the fruit of the individual, but on faith alone, and it is evident that scripture points directly to works. Do not be deceived; every time we make a decision we are sowing a seed for our eternity. Decisions of obedience, forgiveness, judgment, sowing pain in others, and bearing bad fruit. Our job is to help one another in every way shape or form, obedience to the best of our ability, and to uplift and encourage each other.

3. According To Deeds

Romans 2

Who will render to every man according to his deeds: To them who by patient continuance in well doing seek for glory and honor and immortality, eternal life: But unto them that are contentious, and do not obey the truth, but obey unrighteousness, indignation and wrath. **6-8 KJV**

A focus of eternity and immorality is judged by your works in this life. There are no excuses for discouragement. There is no excuse for blatant disobedience and unrighteousness. There is no excuse for bad fruit in this life.

Matthew 7

A good tree cannot bear bad fruit, nor can a bad tree bear good fruit. Every tree that does not bear good fruit is cut down and thrown into the fire. Therefore by their fruits you will know them. **18-20 NKJV**

You will know a true Christian based on their actions. The love in their heart will show in the way they treat others. It will be obvious who the Christians are in this life based on their fruit. A true Christian will be living a Christian life in obedience and love.

4. Final Judgment

During the Lords judgment, if Hell is your destiny, then God will explain to you and show you the disobedience without repentance and the pain you have caused others. He will allow you to feel all of the pain that you have inflected on others. God will explain to you and you will understand that you have been a part of the problem here on earth and you will *both* agree that Hell is what is fair. Then you will have an existence based on the judgment of God that is fair for your deeds.

On the other hand, if you have done your best in obedience, been a light in this world, was an encouragement for the people you came across, focused on your relationship with the Lord, and put Him first in your life, then this will be a good experience because your sin has already been forgiven. God will be showing you all of the good that you have done and explain to you how much help you have given Him. You will be welcomed and be written in the Book of Life.

Living like Jesus to the best of our ability is what is necessary. If you have no regret when you sin, you must rededicate your life to the Lord. We live in a fallen world and no one is perfect, but we can seek to become as close to perfection as possible. Seek the Lord with all of your heart and when you stumble, you must repent and continue to do your best. This is our cycle in life as a true follower of the Lord.

Genesis 3:19 Tanakh

יט עָפָר-כִּי לֻקָּחְתָּ מִמֶּנָּה כִּי, הָאֲדָמָה-אֶל שׁוּבְךָ עַד, לֶחֶם תֹּאכַל ,אַפֶּיךָ בְּזֵעַת
אַתָּה, וְאֶל-עָפָר תָּשׁוּב.

ACKNOWLEDGMENTS

I WOULD LIKE to acknowledge my Editor and beautiful daughter, Krisalyn Ramos. She has been an essential asset in molding this book into what it has become. I am very proud of Krisalyn and all of the accomplishments of her life thus far.

REFERENCES

Definition for Deductive Argument from the Internet Encyclopedia of Philosophy (A Peer Reviewed Academic Resource)

Definition for Inconsistency Fallacy found on Study.com website

Pictures From Dreamstime.com

Scripture From The Bible In Different Bible Translations